W9-BCX-857

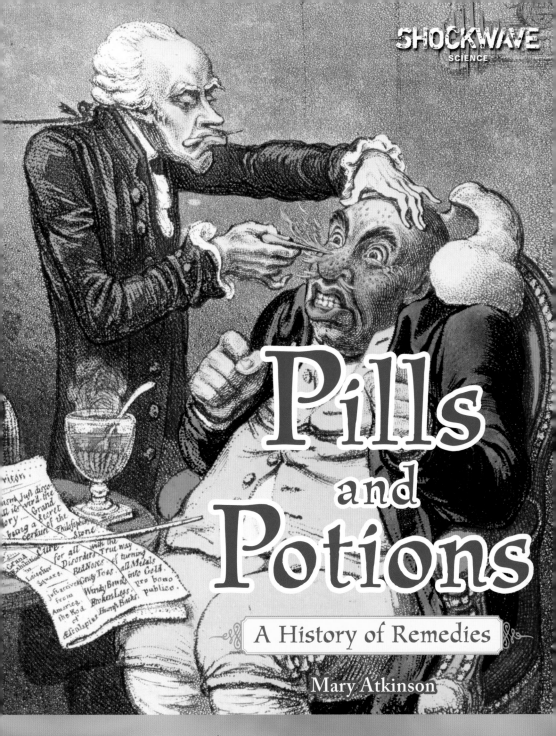

SHOCKWAVE
SCIENCE

Pills and Potions

A History of Remedies

Mary Atkinson

children's press®

An imprint of Scholastic Inc.

NEW YORK • TORONTO • LONDON • AUCKLAND • SYDNEY

MEXICO CITY • NEW DELHI • HONG KONG

DANBURY, CONNECTICUT

Library of Congress Cataloging-in-Publication Data

Atkinson, Mary, 1966-
 Pills and potions : a history of remedies / by Mary Atkinson.
   p. cm. -- (Shockwave)
 Includes index.
 ISBN-10: 0-531-17767-X (lib. bdg.)
 ISBN-13: 978-0-531-17767-9 (lib. bdg.)
 ISBN-10: 0-531-18839-6 (pbk.)
 ISBN-13: 978-0-531-18839-2 (pbk.)
 1. Medicine--History--Juvenile literature. I. Title. II. Series.

 R133.5.A85 2008
 610--dc22

2007018173

Published in 2008 by Children's Press, an imprint of Scholastic Inc.,
557 Broadway, New York, New York 10012
www.scholastic.com

SCHOLASTIC, CHILDREN'S PRESS, and associated logos are trademarks
and/or registered trademarks of Scholastic Inc.

08 09 10 11 12 13 14 15 16 17
10 9 8 7 6 5 4 3 2 1

Printed in China through Colorcraft Ltd., Hong Kong

Author: Mary Atkinson
Educational Consultant: Ian Morrison
Editor: Mary Atkinson
Designer: Amy Lam
Photo Researcher: Jamshed Mistry

Photographs by: **Big Stock Photo** (boy sneezing, p. 25; pills, p. 27); **Getty Images** (p. 8; woman
with skull, p. 9; p. 12; Egyptian women, p.13; Elizabeth Blackwell, p. 25; p. 28; microsurgery,
p. 29); **Jennifer and Brian Lupton** (pro and con teenagers, pp. 30–31); **Photolibrary** (cover; p. 1
p. 11; Edwin Smith Papyrus, p. 13; De Materia Medica, p. 15; Al-Razi, p. 17; pp. 18–19; nurse
washing, p. 23; World War 1 hospital, p. 25; Alexander Fleming, p. 27); **Stock.Xchng** (p. 3);
Tranz/Corbis (pp. 5–7; James Lind, p. 9; p. 10; Kosher Pizzeria, p. 13; p. 14; Roman baths, p. 15
medieval apothecary, p. 17; pp. 20–22; early operating theater, p. 23; p. 24; p. 26; MRI testing,
p. 29; doctor and patient, pp. 30–31)

All illustrations and other photographs © Weldon Owen Education Inc.

CONTENTS

anesthetic (*an iss THET ik*) a drug or gas that prevents
a patient from feeling pain. Some anesthetics make
a person unconscious, or unable to see, feel, or think.

diagnose to figure out what illness a patient has

immunity the body's ability to fight off a particular disease

physician (*fuh ZISH uhn*) a medical doctor

prescribe to write an official note, or prescription,
telling a pharmacist which drugs to give a patient

surgery medical treatment that involves cutting the body

vaccination inoculation of a person with a dead
or weakened form of a germ in order to build up
a person's immunity to a particular disease

· ·

For easy reference, see Wordmark on back flap.
For additional vocabulary, see Glossary on page 32.

The word *anesthetic* comes
from the Greek word *anaisthesia*.
The prefix *an-* means "without,"
and *aisthesia* means "feeling."

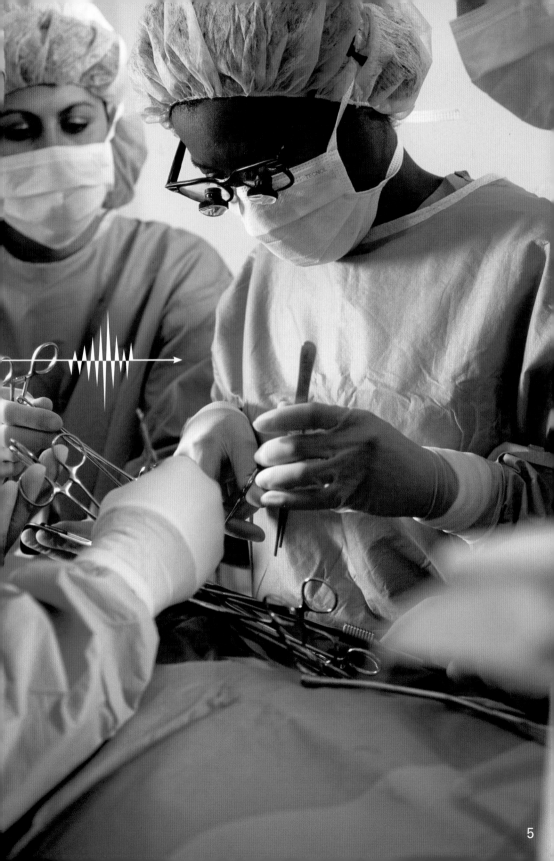

Staying healthy has always mattered to people. Even in prehistoric times, people all around the world searched for the secrets to good health. Some invoked gods and spirits. They devised all kinds of magic charms and healing ceremonies. Others ground up leaves, seeds, and flowers to make their own pills and potions. Some even ventured into **surgery**. Over time, people began to notice which treatments worked and which didn't. People developed increasingly sophisticated health-care systems. However, only in the last few centuries have we begun to understand the causes of many diseases. Medicines such as antibiotics have been around for less than a century. Even today, new advances are constantly being made. Fifty years from now, we may look back and think that the early 2000s were unenlightened times indeed.

Time Line of Medicine

8000s B.C.	1600s B.C.	400s B.C.	1543 A.D.
The earliest-known surgery is performed. It involves cutting holes in a patient's skull.	An ancient Egyptian medical textbook is written. It tells doctors how to treat injuries.	Hippocrates in ancient Greece suggests that diseases have natural causes.	Italian Andreas Vesalius publishes the first book about human **anatomy** based on extensive **observation**.

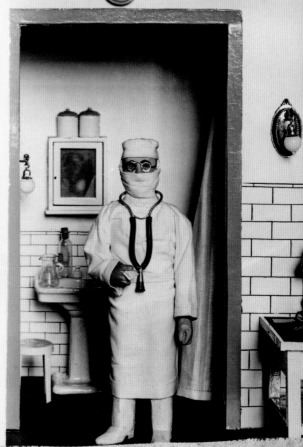

These scenes were created as 3-D models for a World's Fair in 1938. Together, they show a **medieval** doctor alongside a surgeon from the 1900s. They remind us that different things appear strange to us depending on when and where we live. Either doctor could look frightening to someone who was unfamiliar with him.

1840s	1865	1895	1970s	1980s
Two Americans, William Morton and Crawford Long, discover the first **anesthetic**.	English surgeon Joseph Lister founds **antiseptic** surgery. He uses carbolic acid to kill germs.	German scientist Wilhelm Roentgen discovers that X-rays can be used to view bones.	Magnetic Resonance Imaging, or MRI, is invented. It allows doctors to view soft body tissues.	Microsurgery is developed. Surgeons can perform some operations without making large cuts.

First Medicines

No one knows for sure when people first made medicines. Prehistoric people probably noticed that particular plants and animal products had certain effects on the body. For example, thousands of years ago, the ancient Egyptians used honey to prevent infections. Some scientists today believe that honey can kill **bacteria**. The ancient Egyptians may have discovered this accidentally when some honey was spilled on a wound.

Some of the medicines that we use today come from herbs used in traditional medicines for thousands of years. People in ancient Greece used willow leaves and bark to relieve pain and reduce fevers. Today, **pharmaceutical** companies make the active ingredient in willow artificially. It is sold as aspirin.

I misread the word *plants* on the second line. I thought it was *planets*. As soon as I read the word *animal*, I knew I had it wrong. It was obviously *plants*. So I went back and reread, just to maintain the meaning.

In many places, such as South Africa (above), it is customary for a few people in a community to become experts in herbal and other remedies. These traditional healers often use knowledge that has been passed down from one healer to another for centuries. Many traditional healers see no separation between the physical and spiritual health of a person.

In 1535, some French sailors exploring Canada developed **scurvy**. They were cured by Native Americans, who gave them a remedy made from the resin of a spruce tree. In 1753, British **physician** James Lind (center) published a cure for scurvy – citrus fruit. He got some of his information from reading about the French sailors' experience.

SHOCKER

It is thought that about 80 percent of the world's people still rely mainly on herbal medicines. However, they don't always do so by choice. Often it is all the patient can access or afford.

Ancient medical practices sometimes included surgery. In places such as China and Peru, skulls as much as 10,000 years old have been found with holes cut in them. Some holes have started to heal, showing that the patients survived the surgery. The holes may have been made to relieve headaches or prevent seizures.

India and China

In some places, sophisticated medical practices began developing long ago. In India, a medical system called Ayurveda (*eye ur VAY duh*) has been in use for thousands of years. The first Ayurvedic medical school began in about 800 B.C. The students studied many things, including surgery and how to create medicines from herbs and minerals. Many aspects of Ayurvedic medicine are still practiced. Ayurvedic treatments involve balancing five main elements that are believed to make up the body: air, water, fire, earth, and space.

Both Ayurvedic and Chinese doctors feel a patient's pulse to help **diagnose** illnesses. Modern western doctors also feel a patient's pulse to check how quickly, strongly, and evenly the patient's heart is beating.

I can tell by the heading and illustrations that these pages will be about the history of medicine in India and China. It often helps to have a quick scan of a page before reading the text.

Did You Know?

At the site of the ancient Indian city of Harappa, archaeologists have found bones that show signs of surgery and dentistry. This tells us that such practices were occurring at least 3,500 years ago.

In China, by about 500 B.C., the practices of medicine and religion were no longer linked. Some Chinese medicines are based on the idea that illnesses happen when two universal forces, yin and yang, are out of balance in the body. This is thought to prevent energy, called chi, from flowing through the body as it should.

Both Chinese and Ayurvedic **practitioners** consider a person's lifestyle, diet, and other factors when making a diagnosis.

Acupuncture is a traditional Chinese medical treatment. Fine needles are inserted into the skin at particular points. This is intended to alter the flow of energy in the body and so restore health.

One branch of Chinese medicine is based on the idea that there are five basic elements: earth, fire, water, wood, and metal. Combinations of herbal medicines are used to balance these elements in the body.

Fire

Wood

Earth

Water

Metal

In ancient China, medicine was one of the few professions open to women. Today, there are many Chinese woman doctors working in both traditional medicine (above) and western medicine.

Ancient Egypt and the Middle East

In Egypt, medical practices have existed for thousands of years. Imhotep (*Ihm HOH tep*), who lived in about 2650 B.C., is the world's earliest-known physician. After his death, he was revered as a god. Ancient Egyptian writings show that physicians, such as Imhotep, knew a great deal about anatomy and surgery. They wrote about how to treat broken bones, wounds, and some tumors. Their writings describe how to examine, diagnose, and treat an injured patient. They even give information about the **prognosis** of some illnesses. Many other ancient Egyptian writings deal mainly with using magical spells for healing.

Imhotep was a physician and an architect to Pharaoh Djoser. His name means "the one who comes in peace."

Did You Know?

Like modern doctors, some ancient Egyptian physicians specialized in areas such as the eyes or the digestive system.

Ancient Egyptian Physicians
- knew about anatomy and surgery
- wrote about treatments
- gave information about prognoses
- specialized in different areas of medicine

Other Mediterranean peoples also had medical practices. The ancient Israelites had many laws that helped prevent disease. These included isolating people with infectious illnesses and preparing foods according to certain guidelines. Many Jewish people still obey the laws followed by the ancient Israelites. Food that meets all these standards is called kosher food.

This ancient Egyptian document is known as the *Edwin Smith* **Papyrus**. It was written about 1600 B.C., but it is believed to come from much older sources. It is the world's oldest known medical textbook.

SHOCKER

Dead mice were a common ingredient in many ancient Egyptian remedies.

KOSHER PIZZA

A modern Egyptian doctor (right) with a nurse and a patient

Egypt has a long history of female doctors. The earliest known woman physician was called Peseshet. She lived in Egypt about 4,500 years ago. She was also a director of other female physicians.

Ancient Greece and Ancient Rome

Modern western medicine can be traced back to ancient Greece. The Greek god Asclepius (*Uh SKLEE pee uhss*) was the god of healing. Sick people visited his temples to seek cures. In ancient Greece, people believed that all things are made up of four elements: fire, air, earth, and water. The philosopher Hippocrates (*Hi PAH kruh teez*) related the four elements to four bodily fluids, or humors, which he called blood, phlegm (*FLEM*), yellow bile, and black bile. Hippocrates lived in the 400s B.C. He was the first Greek physician to view illness as separate from religion. He stressed that observation and note taking were important.

Asclepius is traditionally shown holding a staff with a snake wrapped around it. The image of the staff and snake is the symbol of the modern medical profession.

The ancient Romans did little to advance medicine. However, they did much to improve public health. The ancient city of Rome had public baths, sewage systems, and clean water flowing through pipes. Claudius Galen (*GAY luhn*) was a Turkish physician living in ancient Rome in the 100s A.D. He believed that illnesses were caused by imbalance of the four humors. He performed experiments on animals to learn more about anatomy, and he wrote many books. His ideas, many of them incorrect, had a huge influence on European medicine up until the 1600s.

The ancient Romans took their health practices with them when they conquered other places. This ancient Roman bath is in the city of Bath, in England.

Similarities Between Ancient Indian, Chinese, and Greek Medical Beliefs

- the body is composed of 4 or 5 elements
- imbalance causes illness
- goal is to achieve balance
- herbal remedies used to restore balance

In 65 A.D., Greek-born Roman doctor Dioscorides (*Dye uh SKOR ih dees*) wrote a book about herbal medicine. It was called *De Materia Medica* (*The Materials of Medicine*). It described the medical uses of about 600 plants and was used in Europe until the 1600s. This illustration comes from an Arabic edition of the book.

Precious Knowledge

In the history of medicine, much information has been lost. Some medical breakthroughs made in the last few centuries were discovered or discussed long before that, but the information was destroyed or not recognized as important. In Alexandria, in Egypt, there was once a vast library of scientific and medical information. Some say that as many as half a million scrolls were lost when the library burned down in the 200s A.D.

When the Western Roman Empire fell in the 400s A.D., many more documents were lost. However, the eastern half of the Roman Empire was not destroyed. Some of the documents in this part of the world survived. They were later read and translated by Jewish and Arab physicians. Eventually, in the late Middle Ages, Arab texts were translated into **Latin** and returned to Europe. Then, during the **Renaissance**, European physicians began building on the knowledge once again.

The Eastern Roman Empire was later called the Byzantine Empire. It was controlled from the city of Constantinople (left), now Istanbul, in Turkey. The empire included parts of Europe, northern Africa, and the Middle East.

Al-Razi (865–925 A.D.) was a Persian physician. He believed in observation rather than guesswork. He suggested that his own observations were more correct than the writings of people such as Hippocrates. He observed and wrote books about many diseases, such as smallpox.

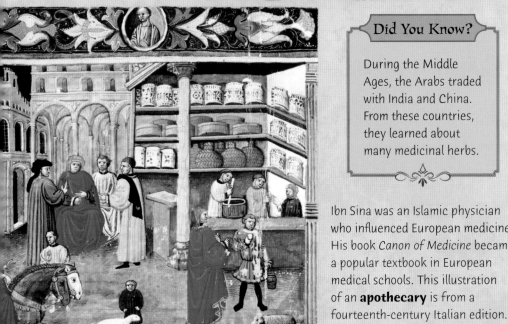

Ibn Sina was an Islamic physician who influenced European medicine. His book *Canon of Medicine* became a popular textbook in European medical schools. This illustration of an **apothecary** is from a fourteenth-century Italian edition.

Lost Knowledge

In 36 B.C., Roman Marcus Varro wrote that creatures too small to be seen can cause diseases. It wasn't until 1546 that another person recorded such an idea. Girolamo Fracastoro, an Italian physician, suggested that diseases are caused by "invisible seeds."

In the first century A.D., Greek physician Soranus worked out safely how to deliver babies that need to be born feet first. This information was rediscovered by Ambroise Paré in 1572.

In 1240, Islamic physician Ibn al-Nafis correctly worked out how blood flows between the heart and lungs. Western medicine did not make this discovery until the 1550s, when it was made by Spaniard Michael Servetus and Italian Realdo Colombo.

The Renaissance

During the Renaissance, European physicians began challenging old ideas and coming up with new ones. Instead of relying on ancient texts, people used more scientific methods to investigate medicine for themselves. The first European medical schools were set up. Old rules prohibiting the dissection of the human body were lifted, and people began studying the body in detail. In 1543, Belgian physician Andreas Vesalius published the first reasonably accurate book on anatomy. It was called *De Humani Corporis Fabrica* (*On the Structure of the Human Body*). It corrected many errors made by Galen. Modern anatomy textbooks are still modeled on this book.

The glossary helped me understand the word *Renaissance*. I remember reading about the Middle Ages. So it makes sense that the Renaissance would follow the Middle Ages. Making connections to what you already know helps you get more out of reading.

Andreas Vesalius

In 1628, English physician William Harvey published his discoveries about human circulation. He was the first person to study all the parts of the process. He realized that the heart pumped blood around the body and back to the heart. His work helped people realize that the best way to understand the body is to study it in detail. It was some time, however, before much of this new knowledge could be put to use. There was no anesthetic, so surgery was painful, and infection still killed many patients. Treatments were mainly the same herbal remedies that had been used for centuries.

SHOCKER

In the 1700s, two popular treatments were bloodletting and a medicine called calomel. This medicine contained mercury, which is a poison. Both treatments were likely to do more harm than good.

European medical books used to be written in Latin. In the 1600s, English herbalist Nicholas Culpeper translated an important medical text into English so that ordinary people could read it. He also wrote a book about the properties of local herbs (left). Other doctors disapproved of Culpeper's work. They wanted medicine to be mysterious, so they could charge high prices.

In the early 1500s, a Swiss physician, Paracelsus (*Par uh SELL suss*), came up with the idea of using minerals, such as sulfur and mercury, as medicines. He also suggested that diseases were not caused by an imbalance of humors, as most people believed.

Surgery and Anesthetics

For centuries, one of the biggest problems with operations was that patients were awake during surgery. Fear and pain made most patients unable to hold still. Some even died of shock. Surgeons tried many ways of calming their patients, such as giving them alcohol or opium. However, these substances had only limited success.

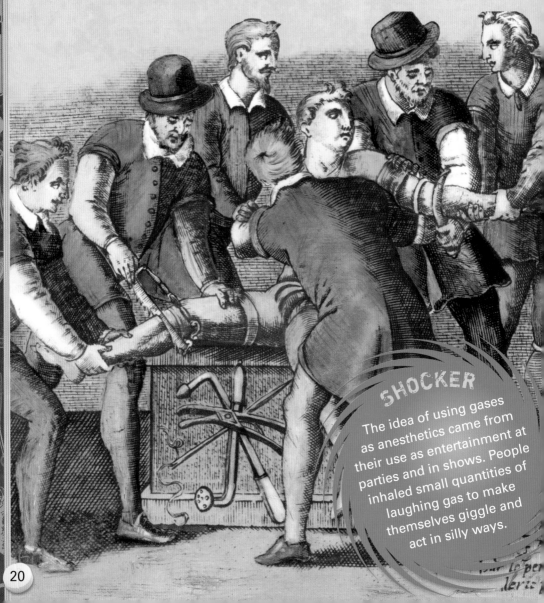

SHOCKER

The idea of using gases as anesthetics came from their use as entertainment at parties and in shows. People inhaled small quantities of laughing gas to make themselves giggle and act in silly ways.

In the 1840s, two Americans discovered that a gas called ether made patients completely **unconscious** for long enough to perform an operation. Ether was the first reasonably safe anesthetic. Dentist William Morton and physician Crawford Long had each made the discovery separately. Suddenly, more people were prepared to have surgery. Surgeons were now able to perform complicated surgery deep inside the body. The range of operations available to patients increased enormously. Soon ether was replaced with another gas called chloroform. This gas had fewer side effects. Today, a range of other drugs are used.

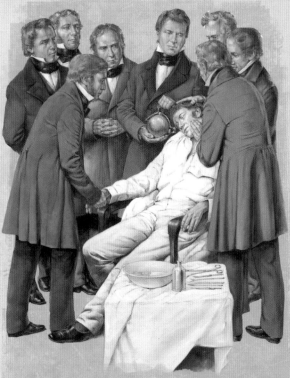

William Morton planned a public demonstration of anesthesia in 1846. When he didn't arrive on time, the audience thought he was a fake. However, after arriving late, he amazed his audience by performing a pain-free operation.

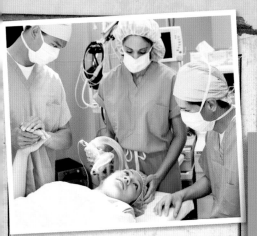

Today, some doctors specialize as anesthesiologists. During surgery, they make sure that a patient always has the right amount of anesthetic in their body.

Did You Know?

Some anesthetics numb only a part of the body. They are called local anesthetics. Dentists often use local anesthetics to numb nerves in teeth before they start drilling.

Without Anesthetic	With Anesthetic
• awake during surgery	• unconscious
• much pain felt	• no pain felt
• simple operations	• more complex operations possible
• shock could kill	• fewer complications

Killing Germs

Even after anesthetics were invented, there was still a big problem with surgery. About 50 percent of patients died from infections in their wounds. People didn't know about germs. Surgeons didn't realize that they needed to wash their hands before operating. Nor did they bother to wear clean clothes.

Then, in 1865, English physician Joseph Lister read the works of French scientist Louis Pasteur. Pasteur's experiments had shown that bacteria can cause decay and disease. Pasteur had figured out that bacteria can be killed with heat or chemicals. Lister started using carbolic acid to kill germs. He washed his tools in it. He also sprayed it on his patients' wounds and in the air. At first, people laughed. But when they saw that 85 percent of Lister's patients survived surgery, they changed their minds. Soon everyone was using antiseptics in surgery.

Lister knew that carbolic acid would kill germs because it was used to clean sewers. It is very strong and stings the skin.

The works of Lister and Pasteur were so important that their names have become household words: *Pasteurized* (heating to kill germs), and *Listerine®* (an antibacterial mouthwash).

In the old days, operating theaters were actual theaters. Large numbers of students would watch operations.

Did You Know?

Today, medical and dental equipment is often heated to a high temperature before it is used. This process kills most germs.

Modern surgeons and nurses wear sterilized robes and caps. Face masks prevent them from breathing germs onto their patients.

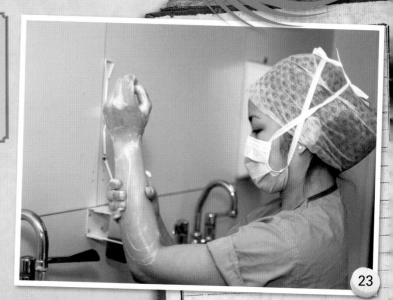

Preventing Diseases

Another person who helped save many lives was Florence Nightingale. In 1854, she traveled from her home in England to a battlefield hospital in Turkey. With a team of 38 nurses, she washed and cleaned both the wards and the patients. She also arranged for bandages and medicines to be sent from England. As a result, the death rate dropped dramatically. She later wrote books and ran campaigns to clean up civilian hospitals. She even set up the first professional training school for nurses.

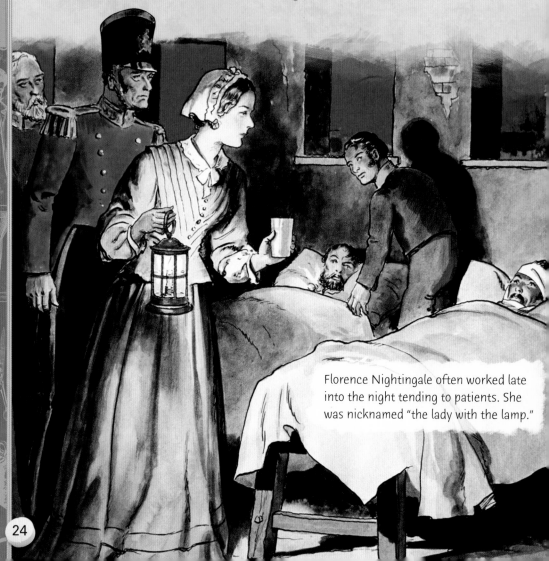

Florence Nightingale often worked late into the night tending to patients. She was nicknamed "the lady with the lamp."

In the 1800s and early 1900s, many women were discouraged from becoming doctors. Some of them became nurses instead. Their work saved many lives, especially in war time.

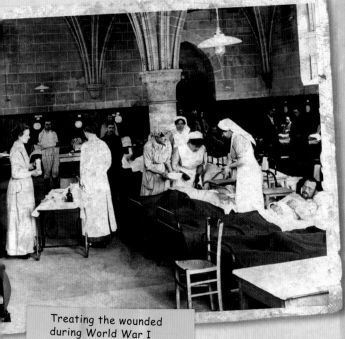

Treating the wounded during World War I

In 1849, Elizabeth Blackwell became the first female doctor in the U.S. After much struggle getting accepted into medical school, she graduated at the top of her class. She later founded a hospital for the poor in New York City.

Once people knew about germs, far more illnesses could be prevented. People were encouraged to wash regularly and use soap. Governments realized the need for clean water supplies and for good sewage systems. People became aware of the link between poverty and poor health. More efforts were made to clean up slum areas and to educate people about hygiene.

How Can You Prevent Diseases from Spreading?

✔ Wash your hands regularly with warm, soapy water – especially before you eat.

✔ Avoid putting your hands in your eyes or mouth. This helps prevent germs from entering your body.

✔ Cover up when you sneeze, and use a handkerchief or tissue.

✔ Avoid sharing drinks with other people. Sharing drinks can spread diseases, such as meningitis.

Vaccinations and Antibiotics

Two further advances transformed medicine. The first was **vaccination**. In 1796, English physician Edward Jenner discovered how to prevent the deadly disease smallpox. He infected people with a related but less severe disease called cowpox. This made people **immune** to smallpox.

In the 1800s, Louis Pasteur discovered how to vaccinate people against other diseases. He figured out that a person could be vaccinated against a particular disease by using weakened or dead bacteria that cause that disease. People infected with weakened or dead bacteria build up **immunity**. They are unlikely to become seriously ill if they encounter the disease later in life.

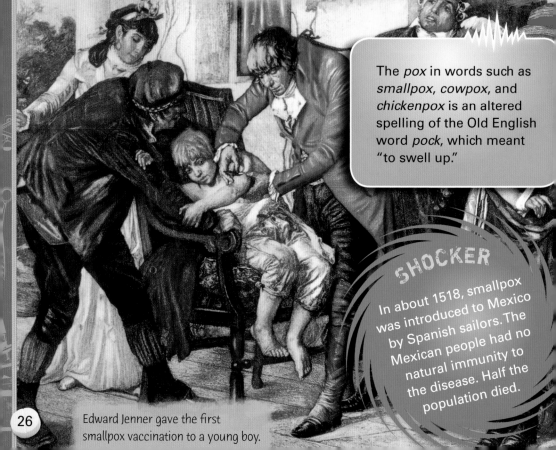

The *pox* in words such as *smallpox*, *cowpox*, and *chickenpox* is an altered spelling of the Old English word *pock*, which meant "to swell up."

SHOCKER

In about 1518, smallpox was introduced to Mexico by Spanish sailors. The Mexican people had no natural immunity to the disease. Half the population died.

Edward Jenner gave the first smallpox vaccination to a young boy.

In the early 1900s, Scottish doctor Alexander Fleming noticed that a particular fungus killed bacteria. Other scientists used this information to create antibiotic medicines. These are medicines that kill specific bacteria. At first, antibiotics were seen as wonder drugs because they cured many deadly diseases, such as tuberculosis. However, some bacteria are now becoming **resistant** to antibiotics.

Things You Should Know About Antibiotics

✔ If you are **prescribed** antibiotics, it is important to finish the course. This will prevent some germs from surviving and becoming resistant to the drug.

✔ Antibiotics cannot cure a cold or flu. These illnesses are caused by viruses. Antibiotics kill only bacteria.

✔ Some people are allergic to antibiotics. If you have a reaction to an antibiotic, call your doctor immediately.

✔ Antibiotics can kill healthful bacteria as well as harmful ones. Take antibiotics only if your doctor prescribes them.

Did You Know?

People develop immunity naturally. If you have already had a disease, such as mumps or chicken pox, you are unlikely to get it again. If you do, it will probably be a very mild case.

Modern Medicine

Some important advances in medicine have allowed doctors to see inside the body without cutting into it. This was first achieved back in 1895, when Wilhelm Roentgen discovered that X-rays could be used to create images of the bones inside a living person. For the first time, doctors could see without operating whether a bone was broken. Since then, other kinds of scans have been developed. In the 1970s, Magnetic Resonance Imaging, or MRI, was invented. MRI images show soft tissues, such as the brain, as well as bones. MRI also has the advantage of being safer than X-ray imaging, because it does not use harmful radiation.

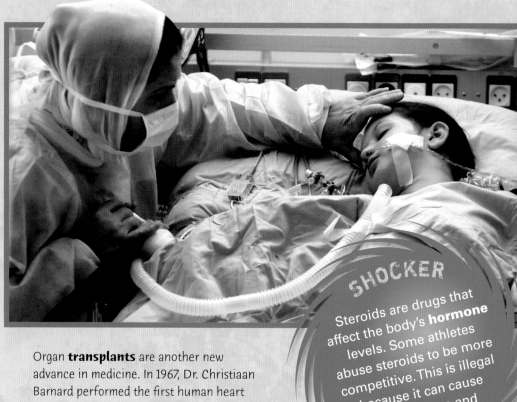

Organ **transplants** are another new advance in medicine. In 1967, Dr. Christiaan Barnard performed the first human heart transplant, in South Africa. Since then, this surgery has saved the lives of thousands of people with heart disease, such as twelve-year-old Samah Gadban (above).

SHOCKER

Steroids are drugs that affect the body's **hormone** levels. Some athletes abuse steroids to be more competitive. This is illegal because it can cause heart disease and other illnesses.

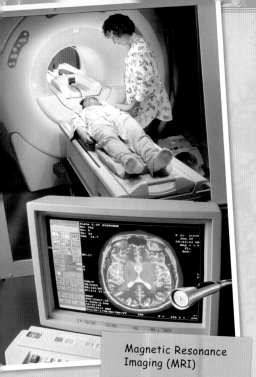

In the 1980s, doctors developed microsurgery. A thin, flexible tube containing a tiny microscope is inserted into the body. Surgeons view the microscope image on a screen. They can then insert tiny instruments into the body through the tube. Microsurgery results in much fewer and smaller cuts to the body than ordinary surgery. The body heals faster, and the patient feels less pain after the operation.

Magnetic Resonance Imaging (MRI)

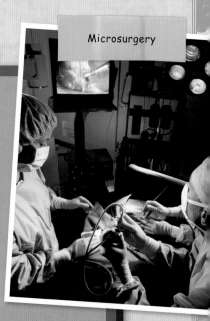

Microsurgery

Careers in Health Care and Medicine

Today, there are hundreds of different jobs available in the fields of medicine and health care. Here are just a few.

eneral practitioners, GPs, are the family octors we visit when we eel unwell. GPs often refer atients to specialists.

Specialists are doctors who have done extra study in specific areas, such as heart disease or bone repair.

Psychiatrists are doctors who specialize in mental health.

Nurses do much of the day-to-day work of caring for patients. Among many other things, they vaccinate people and give health advice.

Some health-care workers, such as **radiologists**, **dietitians**, and **occupational therapists**, work alongside surgeons and nurses in hospitals.

Pharmacists sell drugs and give advice on health-care issues.

Some people work in other areas of health care. For example, they may work in traditional Chinese medicine or as experts in herbal remedies.

29

There is much debate about who is responsible for health care – the patients or the government. In the United States, many people take out **medical insurance** to pay for their own health care. However, this insurance is expensive, too. Millions of Americans cannot afford to pay for it.

WHAT DO YOU THINK?

Do you think people should pay for their own health care?

PRO

People should take responsibility for their own health. If health care were free, people would go to doctors all the time for small aches and pains. This would use up valuable time and money. Also, it is not fair to make rich people pay taxes to help support poorer people.

In some countries, such as Britain, health care is free. However, a high standard of free health care is expensive for a government. This can lead to higher taxes. Some wealthy people in Britain choose to take out medical insurance so that they can have private health care. But they still have to pay taxes to help out those who use the free health-care system.

CON

I think health is vital to happiness. Health care should be paid for by the government. It's not fair if only rich people can afford to be healthy. Some people cannot help it if they are poor. If they are sick and can't afford medicine, they won't be able to get work and help themselves.

Go to **www.bam.gov** to learn more about medicine and health.

GLOSSARY

anatomy the bodily structure of a plant or an animal

antiseptic a chemical that kills germs and prevents infection

apothecary (*uh POTH uh kair ee*) someone who makes and sells medicines; a pharmacist

bacteria (*bak TEER ee yuh*) tiny living things too small to be seen without a microscope

dietitian a person who advises people on diet and nutrition

hormone a chemical produced by a gland in the body that controls body processes

immune able to fight off a particular disease

Latin the language of the ancient Romans

medical insurance an agreement in which a person pays money to a company that agrees to pay that person's medical bills

medieval (*med ee EE vuhl*) to do with the Middle Ages

observation close examination of and attention to something

occupational therapist a person who helps people with illnesses or disabilities recover, develop, or maintain practical skills

papyrus (*puh PYE ruhss*) a reed-like water plant, or the paper-like writing material made from it

pharmaceutical (*far muh SU tic il*) referring to the developing, producing, and selling of medicines

practitioner a person, such as a doctor, who practices a particular kind of medicine

prognosis the chances of recovery from a particular illness

radiologist a health-care professional who takes X-rays, MRI scans, and other scans

Renaissance (*REN uh sahnts*) a period in European history that lasted from the 1300s until about 1600. It was marked by advances in art, literature, and science.

resistant able to survive the effects of a particular drug

scurvy (*SKUR vee*) a disease caused by a lack of vitamin C

transplant to take an organ or tissue from one person and place it in another person

unconscious not conscious; unable to see, feel, or think

INDEX